Mike Honeycutt's World of Hunting and Fishing

MIKE HONEYCUTT

Order this book online at www.trafford.com
or email orders@trafford.com

Most Trafford titles are also available at major online book retailers.

© Copyright 2018 Mike Honeycutt.

All rights reserved. No part of this publication may be reproduced, stored in a retrieval system, or transmitted, in any form or by any means, electronic, mechanical, photocopying, recording, or otherwise, without the written prior permission of the author.

Print information available on the last page.

ISBN: 978-1-4907-8926-2 (sc)
ISBN: 978-1-4907-8927-9 (hc)
ISBN: 978-1-4907-8925-5 (e)

Library of Congress Control Number: 2018946886

Because of the dynamic nature of the Internet, any web addresses or links contained in this book may have changed since publication and may no longer be valid. The views expressed in this work are solely those of the author and do not necessarily reflect the views of the publisher, and the publisher hereby disclaims any responsibility for them.

Our mission is to efficiently provide the world's finest, most comprehensive book publishing service, enabling every author to experience success. To find out how to publish your book, your way, and have it available worldwide, visit us online at www.trafford.com

Any people depicted in stock imagery provided by Getty Images are models,
and such images are being used for illustrative purposes only.
Certain stock imagery © Getty Images.

Trafford rev. 06/13/2018

 www.trafford.com

North America & international
toll-free: 1 888 232 4444 (USA & Canada)
fax: 812 355 4082

CONTENTS

Chapter 1	Northern Cameroon, January 1997	1
Chapter 2	Southern Cameroon, March 1999	4
Chapter 3	Elk Hunting around the Rockies	9
Chapter 4	Northern BC for Moose, 1999	18
Chapter 5	Mongolian Elk or Siberian Elk Hunt	21
Chapter 6	New Zealand, 2001	30
Chapter 7	Córdoba, Argentina, 2001	32
Chapter 8	Old Mexico Turkey Hunting, 2001	35
Chapter 9	South Africa, 2002	38
Chapter 10	Tajikistan, November 2002, Marco Polo	42
Chapter 11	Mongolia, 2003, Gobi Desert	45
Chapter 12	Kamchatka, Russia, September 2004	49
Chapter 13	Zimbabwe, 2005, Dangerous Game Hunt	52
Chapter 14	Polar Bear Hunting on the Polar Ice Pack, 2006	59
Chapter 15	Second Dangerous Game Safari, Eighteen Days in Zambia, 2008	64
Chapter 16	Caribou, Wolf and Fishing, Manitoba September 2009	68
Chapter 17	North Island, New Zealand, 2010	74
Chapter 18	Australia, Hunting Buffalo, 2011	78
Chapter 19	Idaho Cow and Elk Hunting, August 2012	84
Chapter 20	Hunting and Working, New Zealand, April 23, 2013	88
Chapter 21	Elk Hunting, Quebec, Canada, 2013	92
Chapter 22	Botswana, September 2015, Elephant Hunt	96
Chapter 23	September 13-28, 2017	104
Chapter 24	Travel to Canada for a Fishing Trip in June 2004	106

Chapter 25 110
Chapter 26 114
Chapter 27   Another Trip South of the Border to the
              Amazon Region..121

Acknowledgment.. 131

CHAPTER 1

Northern Cameroon, January 1997

I have always had a passion to hunt and travel to other lands. Growing up in a small town, I always had access to land and rifles to hunt with. My family always had land to hunt on and started acquiring acreage early. I became more of an avid hunter for deer, turkey, and quail. After high school, I did a couple of years of college and began to think about hunting different species of animals and traveling to other land. I finally got a chance to travel and hunt for the elusive Lord Derby eland.

I arrived in Paris, France, for an overnight stay. I decided to go sightseeing from my airport hotel. I went downstairs to ride the airport train into Paris, but the security forces were guarding the train gates with machine guns. The train was headed in with suspicious luggage believed to be carrying a bomb, so I had to take a taxi to the subway where I traveled underground all over Paris.

In the evening, the bomb threat was over, and I was able to take the train back to the airport to my hotel. I had dinner and stayed overnight. I arrived at the airport the next day, watching the time as I was already confused with time changes. We took off and landed early morning in Lagos, Nigeria, where the oil workers got off the plane. Most had a month on and a month off, so they flew back and forth to Paris. As the flight attendants opened the door, they told us to sit on the plane while they served coffee and cookies to the military as they came to greet the plane. After loading and unloading freight and luggage, we took off again and headed for our final destination in Douala, Cameroon. Air France had great food and music from Radio Mecca, but their old love story movies were kind of boring. Nigeria and Cameroon were having problems and were fighting and shooting at each other's oil wells out in the ocean. Arriving in Douala, I was booked at the Hotel Meridian. I spent the night having a relaxing evening and dinner and then went back to the airport the next morning to fly north with the other hunters from New York.

Landing in the north on the afternoon flight, we we're driven to camp for a fifteen-day hunt. The camp consisted of getting acquainted and a visit to the sleeping quarters made of concrete and steel doors with grass roofs to keep the lions out. The only other thing we encountered were large spiders that the Danish outfitter suggested help keep out snakes, such as the black mamba, one of Africa's deadliest snakes. As the saying goes, if you get bitten by a mamba, they bypass the hospital and head directly to the morgue.

Cameroon is a savanna in the north and is close to Nigeria's border. The 144 tribes of Islamic fundamentalists live there. One of the young chieftains was one of my guides. They drink and eat only at night. As it turned dark, they would get off the safari rig and pray and eat on the way to camp. One of the men drank his dinner from a mobile oil number 2 jug. We returned to camp every night, had a drink, sat by the fire, and indulged in conversation about the hunting days. The full moon in Cameroon is the best part of an evening, then a great dinner with fresh salads and bread from the mobile bakery, which was an African lady carrying bread on her back. The soil in the hunting concession was red like Mars. I was able to take several of the species there. A Lord Derby eland was the grand prize for me, but I also took a warthog, red hartebeest, a roan antelope, and some duikers. The hunting and tracking to find the animals were some of the best I have ever seen.

As we were leaving the hunting area, we met the state man and the military leader, shook hands with both in the tall grass, and flew away to the base for transfer to the hotel. Returning to Douala, I decided to shop. The area was full of tourists and high-pressure salesmen. Leaving Cameroon and back to Paris to catch the Concorde was easier than arriving in the first place. At sixty thousand feet and over the coast of France in thirty minutes at Mach 2 to 4, I thought how quick I would arrive home as it took me eight hours on the way over. It would take less than three hours to arrive in New York, so I sat back, had breakfast, and prepared for a quick trip over the ocean to New York. Riding high and fast seemed like the only way to go. The cost of flight was knocked way down as I had ridden first-class Air France all the way around, except for the short flight to Chicago to receive the special fare. The Concorde was way faster, only three hours to New York. When I got to Chicago, there were storms that tied me up for an additional eight hours. Then finally, I was able to go home.

CHAPTER 2

Southern Cameroon, March 1999

After traveling over the ocean and hunting different species of animals and visiting different cultures, my passion to return to Africa was strong. An Arab proverb that I read stated that once you drink from an Arab spring, you will return to drink again; and so I was hooked for a second trip, as I really drank from an Arab well in Cameroon on the first trip. I received a call from the outfitter in Houston, Texas, asking me to go again to acquire the bongo in the southeastern region of Cameroon. The bongo was as elusive a creature as the Lord Derby. They both were found only in three African countries. The broker told me that another hunter had backed out of the hunt and that he would give me a substantial discount for the trip and that I would have the same guides and international outfitter that I already knew as well. This hunt was the first in the region for the year, and the French guide told me that no one had been there this year. So I couldn't resist the adventure of returning to Cameroon plus the adventure to a new area and hunting for the elusive bongo that was only seen in three African countries. The only thing that I was a little nervous about was being next to the country that some henchman had fled to from a neighboring country that had just executed some Americans for not staying away from a gorilla area, and they hadn't caught the killers yet. The border and the river were less than seventy miles away, but once I was there, I forgot about the killers and snakes as I did on the first hunt.

Southern Cameroon was a jungle area, and any walk in the woods had to have a trail cut with machetes. We were hunting in this area with dogs called dingos and with cannibals and not Islamic fundamentalists. There were unknown secrets about the little people, but one was for certain—they ate human flesh. After a certain age, their teeth were sharpened, and they looked like shark's teeth. The French guide had faith in them to hunt the elusive jungle animal called the bongo, an orange striped animal with a brownish red coat and spiral-type horns. The bongo is considered one of the most wanted trophies in Africa. We would gather the cannibals every morning and return late in the day. I asked the guide why they didn't feed their dogs more, and he said that if the dogs gained a lot of weight, the people would eat them.

The timber sector we were in was a twenty-four-hour operation so we had to watch for trucks on the main roads. The Danish outfitter had not built a Lodge yet in the area, so he rented space from the Lebanon timber director where we housed for the trip. There were a heard of goats, and an ape named Tonto lived with the director and their caretaker. Tonto would visit us every day. The director was a nice guy, and he had worries about his family in Lebanon, as Israel war planes were bombing an area where his family lived. Accommodations were simple rooms with two beds and a shower and toilet in one corner in a little room. Dining was done in the outfitters cabin. Good food and blue cheese that was a dessert on Air France was one of my favorites. Since the guide had worked for the French ambassador and the other American was ex-military and a water works director, we had some interesting conversations and sometimes heated disagreements at dinner. Dinner usually went very well, as we were hungry.

After several days of hunting and trying to understand each other, we successfully tagged a bongo—a beautiful animal and a nice trophy. We also hunted Duikers in the jungle but used shotguns for this one. They were small and very quiet runners. There were sitatunga and dwarf buffalo and elephants, but we only saw their tracks. When we first arrived, there were some huts spread through the jungle with poachers setting snares that would catch animals by the foot. The Frenchman would march his men into the huts and try and burn them. We never actually got close to anyone because they left before he got there. The Frenchman was quite an interesting topic of conversation. Once we got through the obstacles such as talking too fast, we had some unusual conversations about Northern Africa such as Yemen. Known for its ability to change things overnight and the training camps for terrorist around the world, it was still a place the French chose to occupy. With his knowledge of working with the ambassadors and connections with royalty in France, there was never a dull moment in the jungle whether it was conversation or actually something going on. Because of the green damp jungle, a hut would only burn a little and go out. One time, we were driving along and came across a one-hundred-foot swath of mangled trees, and I said, "Do you have tornados here?

He replied, "That is from a herd of dwarf elephants." All the trees were mangled and twisted. There was always a need for malaria medicine in Cameroon, and you could just be driving along, or in this case, we were repairing a bridge that had gone out from the earlier flooding on the ditches and roadway. This girl came walking out of the jungle and asked for malaria pills. Of course, no one had a malaria pill supply, as we were hunting. We left the timber district to begin our journey back to Douala to prepare for flight to Paris and, in my case, back on the Concorde to the United States. We stopped a couple of places along the way to pick up computers for repair in Douala and visited with the locals there. At the first place we stopped, we were met by a man wearing a Texaco shirt, and he knew Colonel Kaddafi. Some very interesting people in the jungle and every one had something that needed repaired in the city. We fueled the plane out of a fifty-five-gallon drum and took off for the airport. Arriving in Douala, we were taken to the hotel to clean up and get ready for the international flight to Paris. Arriving in terminal 2 in Paris, I got my boarding pass and sat down to wait for the Concorde. Along came a familiar face with his wife, and they wanted to know where I was from. After a photo, they sat down with me to wait for their plane to Houston, Texas. While I was waiting for a Concorde to New York. The president of the United States and his wife sat with me while watching their son run for president on Paris TV. The flight attendant came by and said they were having labor problems and asked if I would rather take a later plane or fly with less service. Everyone opted to take an early flight with Diet Coke and a sandwich, which was much less glamorous than my first Concorde flight in 1997 with caviar, pancakes, and lobster bisque. Returning home was much easier than the first flight.

CHAPTER 3

Elk Hunting around the Rockies

Taking a break from international hunting, I have to say that elk hunting and the scenery around the Rocky Mountains in the northwest are spectacular in the fall and early winter. I hunted elk for many years in the Bob Marshall wilderness with a group of mostly older hunters, a horseback ride through the Molly Basin, Rampart Mountain. Valley of the Moons, where the grizzlies stood up on their hind legs and marked the trees with their huge claws, Haystack Mountain and the Chinese Wall, camping where the flat and Sun Rivers meet. There were the remains of a New Year's Eve plane crash that took the lives of a family of four heading west. They found the plane in the spring, and they had hit the face of the mountain head-on. Nothing was left of them in the spring. Speculation was that grizzlies had dragged them from the plane and ate their bodies. Pieces of the plane were scattered on the shore of the Sun River. Hunting there was demanding, as the air was thin and the trails were winding, narrow elk trails. I remember one trip where it snowed six inches in the morning and completely cleared in the afternoon. The weather there was usually descent, but it had an ability to change very rapidly. You never knew who you would meet in the mountains as well.

The day it snowed, we divided up and decided to hunt back to camp. I was on a high ridge coming out to a small clearing and had just seen a huge deer go off the mountainside, and as I came out of a dense area to a rise in the terrain, there were three horsemen on their horses looking down at me. I had never seen them before and didn't know how they got there. We had a small talk and parted company, returning to camp. No one seemed to know who they were. The horses were kept in a perimeter at night inside the camp with the tents. One night, a bear came into camp, and we woke up in our tent in a horse stampede. There was never a dull moment in the hunting camps twenty miles and an eight-hour ride in the mountains. One morning, we decided to ride to the continental divide through the pass. We could see a tent just this side of the pass.

Looking below the tent about two hundred yards was a huge grizzly bear. He saw us and turned to run, knocking the aspen trees down. All equipment, horse feed, and food had to be packed on mules and brought in to camp. When we rode back out of the mountains to the ranch in Augusta, Montana, it was about a thirty-two-hour ride back home. We hunted there for twenty years or more until the old outfitter sold the camp and many of us were older, so we decided to find an easier, shorter trail to ride. Our next excursion into the elk hunting arena was out of Lincoln, Montana. Red Mountain and the Scape Goat Wilderness were our next project. We had about the same travel miles of thirty-two hours but different scenery and a fifteen-mile shorter ride into the wilderness on horseback. We always rode the pass into Lincoln from Helena and stopped on the mountain to take photos of the area or just take a break. Little did we know that the Uni Bomber lived above the area that we always stopped. We even knew the law enforcement officer that took him in to custody, but Lincoln was a great place to stay, and the trail where we were hunting was nearby. The supper club in Lincoln served the best steaks I had ever eaten and remained our favorite hangout until it burnt to the ground. I just recently heard that it was rebuilt last year and is serving food again. So there have been other solo elk hunts, but the two areas mentioned have been the best.

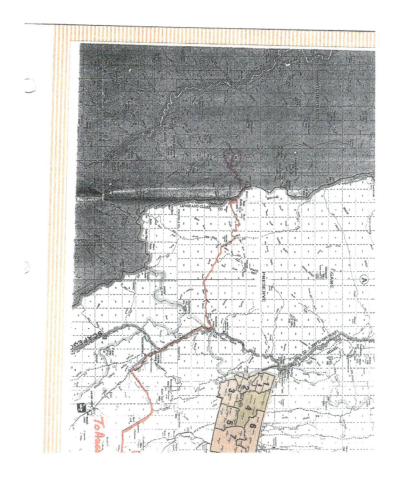

The Chinese Wall from below Cliff Mountain looking north toward the head of Moose Creek.

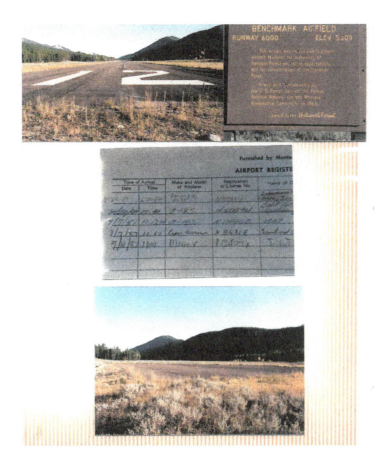

Time of the Elk

BENCH MARK FALL 1988

CHAPTER 4

Northern BC for Moose, 1999

I had almost forgot about this chapter in the hunting diary.

I flew to a mechanized camp for a moose hunt. Being mechanized means it was about the only way to get around, and we rode ATVs. The frozen thawing ground was tricky to move on, and it wasn't walkable. It was like a frozen sponge. We attempted to hunt wolf, and there were bears everywhere. When the soil freezes there, the oil rigs move north to do their work, and the soil is mushy unless it is frozen solid. I landed there by floatplane built to land short and take off very short so you didn't hit a mountain. As the hunt continued, the rules for taking moose, elk, or anything else changed as the hunt progressed. For instance, a moose had to have three prongs on one side. An elk, after a certain date, had to be a six by six. The countryside was beautiful, as trees were changing color every day. At night, in my tent, the elk there were not quite in the rut but bugled all night long. After I got a moose, we flew from the mechanized camp to the main camp that looked like an airport in the wilderness. We proceeded on horseback in the main camp for elk, caribou, and mountain goat, but I was unsuccessful at every attempt, so I sent my moose to taxidermy there to have the head mounted. I flew to Edmonton for the night and back to the States the next day with three hundred pounds of meat. I arrived home the next afternoon.

CHAPTER 5

Mongolian Elk or Siberian Elk Hunt

In 2000–2001, I decided to go on a Mongolian elk hunt. The group that was hunting together had sort of broke up for hunting elk in the United States, so I thought I would give it a try elsewhere. We had several hunters, but the two I remember the most were a salesman from New York and a Navy SEAL from Wyoming. We camped about four hundred miles south of the Russian border. There were several elk there, but distance shooting was tough in that area because you could see as far as you look. I remember the first day we went out, the sky looked funny, but it was clear at a lower elevation. As the guide and I climbed, a blizzard hit us in the face, and we could not even see for several minutes and had to return to a lower elevation. After several days of hunting, we had our quota of elk and was ready to descend the mountain in our Russian jeeps.

We had lunch one time with my driver's family in town as we drove for supplies. If you needed to go to the restroom, you would walk in a building that sits ten feet above ground. You would break you neck if you fell in. There were many friendship areas along the way. People stacked things there such as bottles and cans. The land was barren, rocky, and steep. The gers we stayed in were roomy and warm for three people. The farmers and their camels and yaks roamed the countryside. Once we got our elk, we headed back to Beijing, China, to Miat Airways. I had the honor to sit by the president of the Soviet senate, on his way to Vietnam. We discussed the Great Wall and other points of interest as we eat dinner on the plane to Beijing. Coming to China, we got diverted to Shanghai, not knowing why. We found out that Bin Laden had put a death threat on all people, so the Chinese would not let us in direct. We had some time before going home, so we toured the Great Wall and had Peking duck as well as other Chinese dishes. We toured Tiananmen Square and the Forbidden City and watched the Chinese military march. Then we went to a shop where they opened pearls and made rings or necklaces as finished product. Then it was time to head home, so we did so the next day. When you travel from the West to East, you can travel home the same day because of the time change. When you are leaving to go East to West, it takes two or three days going to Asia. You carry your trophies with you, and you have to pay for weight in kilos. So if you have big heavy horns, it costs quite a bit more. One of our guys had a four-inch knife blade in his pocket. He almost got to reside in China, but our interpreter saved the day.

CHAPTER 6

New Zealand, 2001

I have business interests in New Zealand, so when I can go, I use the trip to include some hunting. This particular trip started in Gisborne for meetings and then a flight to Queenstown for an overnight and a full day's hunting before heading back to the States. I called the booking agent, and he said we can book, but we would be ahead to borrow a gun there because of the short trip. So I booked with the Serbian outfitter, and as I was having dinner, he handed me a pill and said, "You will need this on the chopper in the morning." So we left early, about 4:00 a.m., to meet the chopper. Just after daylight, we pulled in through the gate and into the valley to meet the chopper coming through the valley. He landed and picked me up for a Himalayan tahr hunt in the mountains across Mount Cook.

After several hours into the early afternoon, we had a tahr and went back to camp to begin a red stag hunt. After some time scoping and looking around, I now had my stag and began a late afternoon hunt for fallow buck, but I shot a tree, as the fallow went into a draw, and then it was getting late and time for dinner, out the next morning for travel to the States and back home. Same scenario as Asia—you get up in the morning, and you know that when you cross the equator, you will arrive the same time and day you left. The seasons are in reverse, so if you are in New Zealand in the spring, you will arrive home in the fall or early winter. Confusing enough when you have time changes, let alone packing for summer there and winter here and getting on a transport that limits your luggage. Not so much getting there, but it bottlenecks when you take a domestic flight from an overseas trip on how much you can carry without paying overweight fees. Usually, overseas flights are relaxing, and the service is good. Since I only spent a week in New Zealand each trip, I fly nearly every other day between the north and south island before returning. It is one of the most beautiful countries in the world.

CHAPTER 7

Córdoba, Argentina, 2001

It takes about eight hours to fly from Miami to Buenos Aires. Then we stayed overnight and went to Córdoba, the grain capital and hunting area of Argentina. These grain fields support eighteen million doves and parakeets that destroy acres of grain every year. One parakeet can bite the whole grain head off a milo stalk, so hunting is one way of helping reduce the large numbers of birds. Hunting there is a long day of constant shooting with hot gun barrels that you never touch while firing rapidly. Bird boys are busy loading your gun and serving drinks. We start early and hunt until noon, have lunch and a nap until 3:00 p.m., and then shoot constantly until almost dark, then dinner and bedtime. Most hunts are three days and then home. If you like to shoot, this kind of hunting is the most exciting. One hunt I went on, I was shooting in the trees and saw movement other than birds in the trees. There were people picking up birds in the trees while we were shooting. I told the bird boy, and he said that's normal. They have to be getting popped or touched by my ammo load, but we keep on shooting. Usually, birds are collected and fed to the local hogs and not to people. I never ate a bird while I was there. Argentina's beef is the best in the world—barbequed and served without sauce and is tasty. At home, I would smother beef in sauce and eat all the doves we could hunt, which was minimal compared with hunting in Argentina. The restaurants in Argentina that we used to eat at in Old Mexico and about seventy miles from my house were great. They know how to season meat. We stayed in a former general's estancia, and it was very good accommodations. I remember landing the second trip and visiting with the customs agent while we waited for our guns to clear.

He asked me how many birds we have killed. I remarked ten thousand. He said, "You have to be kidding." He said that they had a group going there next week to hunt. I said, based on what they told me, that amount didn't affect the population at all. Ten thousand out of eighteen million is not many. So there, again, I headed home. That particular trip was a great hunt in that they had new Berettas and new

20-gauge Benelli shotguns that were considered top guns for rapid shooting. The only thing wrong was that they lost my guns at the airport and never could find them, but I ended up with all new guns and a new gun case.

CHAPTER 8

Old Mexico Turkey Hunting, 2001

In 2001, turkey hunting for a World Slam required the two Mexican turkeys: the Gould's turkey, the Ocellated, and the four species in the United States. The Mexican turkeys were located in Sonora out of Hermosillo and Campeche. The outfitter put me up at their lodge in Hermosillo for the night and then proceeded to camp through the pine trees to the hunt. I felt at home in the trees, as I live in the pines at home, but the poverty in town was a typical Mexican scenario: one fancy lodge or hotel and shacks all around them; chickens everywhere. My guide was as good as any guide in the States. He was Mexican and was a great guide but drove his truck in the middle of the road. The curvy, mountainous roads were difficult to maneuver on anyway, but the guide took his half and more. Hunting was exciting, and if a lot of birds came in, you had to pick and choose so you didn't kill too many at one time. The first morning, he threw lots of grain out around the blind and started calling. We had birds gobbling and walking around us for a long time before I could shoot. I met an eye surgeon from Guadalajara, and he had gone to the university there and practiced eye surgery in the United States. He and I were avid hunters, and we decided to fly to the other Mexican turkey on the other end of Mexico in the state of Campeche together so we could talk turkey while we traveled. It took all day to fly from one end of Mexico to the other, and flying from timber and hills to jungle, we went for new terrain to a different species of turkey.

Arriving we gathered our gear, and six people got in a car the size of a Cadillac. It took five hours to get to the hunting lodge. There were chicken coops and shacks. We finally came to the lodge. As we arrived, females from the press were there but leaving. There were firefighters from California and navy people, a doctor and a sniper whom I hunted with about every day and, a marine who told us how to run from killer bees in the jungle. Our accommodations had a picture of a turkey painted on the wall, a refrigerator, tables, and sides up so high, but the wall stopped, and it was open to the roof. Next morning, I went hunting. We left early and were walking in the jungle when a bird screamed. I remember remarking and saying what the hell was that. The hair stood up on the back of my neck, and the guide said, "That is your turkey." We walked about a mile in the jungle. It never got daylight, and he said, "I will laser the limb, and you shoot the turkey." He pushed the button on the laser, and the limb lit up. I couldn't tell which end was which, so he changed position, and I took a shot and got my turkey. Still could not see daylight until we walked out into a field from the jungle. I tried my luck for a brocket deer, but without big horns, I opted to leave the jungle early instead of hunting, thinking I could leave Mexico early to take my trophy out. One day we were hunting Brocket Deer, and a large anteater showed up. That was quite a sight to see, as I had never seen one up close and personal. Then it was time to leave, as I was trying to leave early so my trophy would not spoil, but I was not able to leave Mexico early because of flight scheduling, and carrying bird parts might cause a problem leaving from another state. So I went sightseeing and worked around Campeche. Finally, it was time to head out for Miami and home. I was lucky that my bird was still mountable, as it had to pass customs, a veterinarian, and then to the taxidermist.

CHAPTER 9

South Africa, 2002

I won an auction hunt for leopard at DSC in January 2002 and took off to go to South Africa. The people hunting and visiting in the camp were from the government. Most were from Cape Town and Johannesburg. They wanted to know about 9/11. I was one of the few Americans in their country after 9/11. We stood by the campfire, drinking and talking about the Twin Towers and everything else. Hunting in Northwestern South Africa was much smoother than the earlier hunts in the jungle in terms of terrain, but I was told that we would go out, get a leopard, and be back early for breakfast. At two in the afternoon, we had one leopard, a dog with two huge holes in his back from the leopard bite, and had walked halfway to town. We headed to town to get the dog fixed up and went over to Bush and Bulls for a steak, then returned to camp for what was left of the day. Dinner was interesting, as another group from Greece was there. The ambassador of Greece, a rich hotel operator, and the minister of justice, they had been bird hunting, and I had a leopard, so there was a large variety of different meats served on various grills for dinner. We enjoyed eating, and I remember one of the men asking the host with whom they were good friends what the leopard tasted like, and he remarked it tastes like chicken. So we continued the hunt the next day of the seven-day hunt for waterbuck, and after several hours, we got a nice buck, a great end to another good day on safari. I can't really remember a bad day on safari. The remaining days were spent hunting my quota that I paid for, including the bushbuck.

I had a license for spur-winged goose, Egyptian goose, yellow-billed duck, red-billed teal, and white-faced duck, and we had transferred to the northeast side of Johannesburg about three hours north. We transferred to a lodge in the northeast that had fenced game animals all around us. There were lions behind us that groaned all night the first night and sleep like babies after they were feed the second night. You could have heard a pin drop the second night. There were panthers, tigers, ostrich, and lots of others. The pet caracals were all around us when we walked in the yard. They would sit under bushes and look out at us, and then they would run in the house to the roof and had ways out. I stuck my little finger through a cage in the house, and a lemur with big eyes and small skinny fingers wrapped his fingers around my little finger. I was able to pet a lioness through the fence. After she had helped eat an ostrich, she had blood all over her mouth but was licking herself off in the sun. We were in the grain belt and often got behind big bends of grain going to the mill or storage areas. The farmers were mad that they were having to feed a neighboring country.

I returned to New York, and customs called me in their office and were very angry. I hadn't filled out the famous 4457 form to declare my rifles, but I was able to move on. I always fill that form out when I get ready to leave. I also found out that part of the reason they were alarmed was that there was a warehouse that was stealing guns from the airport and storing them in South Africa. This appeared on television weeks later.

CHAPTER 10

Tajikistan, November 2002, Marco Polo

I am not a high-altitude guy. Even though I did this hunt, it is a misery. You are either trying to get your breath in the frigid air at thirteen thousand to fourteen thousand feet or you are trying to stay warm. The ride there was a long one. One of the hunters lost his sandwich, and nobody had seen it. I thought that somebody probably saw it lying around and ate it, as snacks were scarce. When we got out to stretch, it fell out of the van, and I didn't have the heart to tell him that I stepped on it as I got out of the van in the dark. We bribed every guard house, and there were many. It took a long time to issue bread and vodka to every place. One place we came to on the major highway was closed until 6:00 a.m. because of drug traffic. A machine gun set off to the side was heavily fortified. The guard would step out at daylight and open the gate.

Approaching our destination, we stopped for a break. They had coffee, and it looked like brownies, but the first bite woke me up. It was so sour that I spit it out in my hand. It was a baked camel bar. One of the men from California slipped on the concrete on his way to the bathroom, which was about a number 12 shoe print. After a long break, it was time to roll on in to camp. We slept in an old Russian Observatory with radiated heat. The country was torn apart with the fall of the Russian empire, and camps were left abandoned. The country was run by the communists, Islamic fundamentalists, and other factions. We could only hunt in certain areas. Therefore, a national guided us there the turmoil. We would ride out for the day. Hunting in high-frigid country, some of the sheep we scoped with binoculars could not even be reached. We always stopped at a yak farmer every day to take a break. There was always warm yak milk, sour cream, and butter. In frigid weather, a large bowl of yak milk looked pretty good. After a warm-up, we would hunt along the Afghanistan border and usually find a big open spot for lunch and phone call or whatever. Looking over into Afghanistan, the mountains were high and jagged. We hunted all day, and at dark, since it was Ramadan, the crew would stop and pray a couple of times back to camp. There was a difference in the Islamic fundamentalists in Africa and those we were hunting with in Tajikistan. The Africans only prayed and fed after dark, and where we were hunting, they ate day and night. The Muslims ate only a certain kind of bread and the country had run out of this bread.

On the third day, we saw three rams that were sizable but not extra-large curls, but I decided to take one because hunting is not a sure bet. If you see a good trophy, it is usually smart to take him if you want a trophy to take home and mount on the wall. Most of us left early, but some stayed on to try for a sheep. Several hunters were injured as we drove to camp or during our short stay. The camp manager broke his arm looking for another hunter's sheep. One hunter from California fell on the icy concrete going to the rest room and dislocated this arm. He had to visit army surgeons around Dzhartyrabot. I was shooting at a steeper angle than normal, and my scope sliced the center of my upper nose between the eyes and started bleeding. I was getting ready to go to the surgeons, but the bleeding stopped. Flying back from OSH, one of the hunters suffered a heart problem, and we had to turn him over to surgeons in Bishkek, but he was able to fly on home.

I was meeting a private plane in Chicago, and their intel told me the US Air Force was in Bishkek waiting for a big military operation sometime after the first of the year 2003. When we landed, there were US Jets all around the airport. We were on the northern end of the Himalayas. You could see for twenty miles.

Returning to Bishkek, we spent the night in Istanbul. Sightseeing was fun in Istanbul. I went by the Koran and a Mosque. You could take photos in the Mosque but not of the Koran. It was so old that it was encased in glass. As history says the three main religions crossed paths centuries ago. It was one of the largest books I had ever seen. Shopping was a good pastime while waiting for the International Turkish Air Flight back to Chicago.

On the way to Chicago, I called the jet operator to keep him informed about what time we would land so the jet in Florida could pick me up in Chicago. Every time the Turkish pilots would update the computer screen, I would call and pass the info along to the operator. As we crossed into North America, I called one last time to update the pilots through the operations center. It was perfect timing in Chicago, as they were waiting for me as I cleared customs and turned my sheep over to the broker for clearance to leave. Great flight home. Luckily, the skies were clear, and the Citation X that I asked for had me home very quickly.

CHAPTER 11

Mongolia, 2003, Gobi Desert

I arrived in the Mongolian capital of Ulan Bator. Preparing for a long trip to the Gobi Desert. I had spent the night in Seoul, South Korea, from Tulsa to Dallas to Incheon, Korea, and a fifty-mile bus ride to the Ritz Carlton in Seoul. We bused back to Incheon the next morning for the ride into Ulan Bator via Korean Air, checking to the Genghis Khan Hotel. We began our journey the next day and flew to Dalanzadgad. From there, it was more than an eight-hour drive to the camp near the Chinese border where we stayed in gers as we had done in 2000, only near China instead of Russia to the north. We saw thousands of wild horses on the way to camp. A long journey to the Chinese border, nearly two hours southwest from camp, we hunted closer to camp the first two days and with no luck, so we began a journey through the desert to the Chinese border. There, we pitched tents and began a look out for Gobi Argali sheep. I had a long-range scope to view and loaned it to the scout. He issued Walkie talkies so all the scouts could communicate with him. That area had unusual jagged sharp rock cliffs, and you could see for miles. There was a long valley right on the border, and at the far end was a mountain with a valley in the mountain facing us. We hunted in the afternoon and saw a very good ram that I almost shot at, but because of so many ewes, we couldn't take a safe shot, so we looked for them again until dark and went back to camp.

Earlier in the day, we were sitting on a high cliff and saw three red wolves approaching at a distance toward a tree full of partridge. The wolves scared the partridge out of the trees as they moved through the valley. I didn't shoot because we were still looking for sheep, and anything would spook the sheep away. The second day began the same way. We started out from camp and began scoping and looking at the jagged cliffs when the scout with my scope spotted two sheep lying down in the valley of the big mountain facing us about twenty or so miles away. After looking at them, we decided to drive as far as we could and then climb the mountain. It took almost half a day to get there, so it was early afternoon before we climbed the mountain and were looking down on the sheep. After what seemed like an eternity, the guide motioned to the interpreter to bring me to the rim to have a look. As we sneaked up there and peered over the rim, the sheep started to get up and run. The guide was relaying a message to the interpreter, and she relayed it to me to take the rear sheep, so I fired and dropped the sheep. After taking photos, we carried the sheep down the mountain and started our journey back to main camp so the guide could prepare the sheep for transport to the United States.

The outfitter wanted to explore an area in the southeastern corner of the Gobi near the Chinese border, so she and I took off the next day on a day trip. We looked at a large dinosaur print on our way. We continued onward to the petrified forest park, asking if I could bring some home. She said yes. I paid for an additional twenty pounds of rock at the airport, plus I brought part of a sixteenth-century monastery Home. Great day, almost as much fun as the hunt itself. So we gathered everything up and drove the long road back to the International Visitors Camp. A huge place with everything, we spent the night and then a plane flight to the capital, a weekend there to prepare to fly out, great dining. We ate good food all weekend and went back to Seoul, another night at the Ritz, and then Dallas and home.

CHAPTER 12

Kamchatka, Russia, September 2004

The trip to Kamchatka was one of the shortest trips I ever flew. Circling Petropavlovsk four and a half hours. Several sets of moose horns in the bush later on Magadan Air, submarines were floating in the bay; but at the second go-around, they were all underwater. It reminded me of the movie *The Hunt for Red October*. Crossing from Anchorage was a short ride compared with many other trips out of the United States. The only other thing I knew was the trip back across was the last flight out, and then it would have to be several time zones to Moscow and out to New York if I missed that flight. In the end, we made the last flight out of the year.

We had dinner and loaded up on a bus to the chopper base at Esso, about eight hours from the submarine base. Hunting there was great, lots of game and big moose that we did all the hunting by horseback so you could see their horns in a tall thick bush. I mean that is all you could see of a 1,500-pound moose. Bears were everywhere but couldn't see them in the bush. We were there as the trees were turning color and the bees were still out. The food was the worst I had anywhere, but they didn't have much time to prepare for the hunt. As we were confirmed, the Russians wanted an additional $5,000 per hunter to go to the original camp up north for scouting by chopper. The outfitter said no, and we had already paid a deposit, so he found a new place that an ex-KGB agent owned. We spent the night in a house that was close to the helipad where we would fly out of in the morning. As we arrived at the helipad, the outfitter divided the hunt. I went with one guide from Moscow, and the others went with the outfitter and a longer chopper ride with the other Moscow interpreter. Arriving camp, we all were in the same house and had outdoor restrooms and showers. There were four people in the house, guide, cook, and other help with the interpreter staying in a tent. That evening, we rode into the hunting area where we viewed several sets up moose horns in the bush. Next day, we headed into the hunting area and crossed the river near a hut with windows boarded up from bear attacks.

There were two benches and a table in there and packets of cheese for food. We spent the next night there and started out the next day.

As we made a short trip past the hut near the river, the guide called, and a moose was heading my way in the bush. I got my moose right there. He came in grunting in thick cover. He took the head and some meat and decided to go back to main camp and bring his helper back for the meat the next day. I couldn't speak Russian, and he didn't understand English, and the interpreter didn't go with us, so we had a problem communicating right away. When he called, I put my hands up in the air, and he nodded. We put the head and horns on horses to head to camp, but the horses didn't like meat on their back, and the guide had to lead my horse close to the other horse to get him to move. Arriving, we saw more moose on the way. The place was game rich and very good cover for big animals. I ate dinner and went to bed that night. Third night in camp, pressure was off. I had my moose already and was preparing to try for a bear, but I woke up early morning and drank a lot of water and went back to sleep. I woke up a few minutes later with a real sickness, and it lasted for three or four days. Finally, I was able to carry my gun again and we headed to the river to hunt bear. The salmon were spawning and would go between our feet and swoosh. They told me that one of the US presidents had fished that stream, but the bears were feeding on a night cycle, so we tried a couple of days, but there was no way to break the cycle. We would come to the stream in the mornings and find stripped fish heads and moose legs lying around, so there was nothing to do but quit hunting. I went back to camp, and we walked around. I had brought a pistol, and we took turns shooting. It was almost time for the chopper to stop by and pick me up. We left the chopper base at Esso and returned to the submarine base. Did a lot of sightseeing, ate caviar and salmon from the open market place, drove by the KGB, sightseeing all over the city, went to a brewery, and had potato chips and fresh beer. I remember looking out of the window across the river, and there were Russian tanks playing war games across the water. Had a great dinner and good night's sleep. Prepared to take the last trip out of the city to Anchorage. They suspend the airline flights to Alaska for the season. We had dinner at the airport and flew to Anchorage, Alaska, and then everyone went their own direction. I was headed to Minnesota and on to Bismarck, North Dakota, and on to Pollock, South Dakota, for the week. I arrived at the airport to pick up a rental, as I had seventy miles to drive to my next adventure. By the time we found the rental, it was late, and I arrived at my destination for an hour's rest before going out for the opener of pheasant season.

CHAPTER 13

Zimbabwe, 2005, Dangerous Game Hunt

Trying to get to Zimbabwe with weapons is nearly impossible from the United States when there is an embargo on. The British would not let me fly direct to Harare, the capital of Zimbabwe, in 2005. I had to fly to Johannesburg, South Africa, and then on to Harare. At the same time, the South African carrier was nearly on strike. As the main intercontinental carrier into Africa, they were on the verge of a major shutdown. I didn't want to be stuck somewhere during a strike, so I decided to take my chances with the British. As luck would have it, SAA did go on strike, and I barely made it out to my destination on another British Air flight, but with luck, I was able to get to my destination.

Arriving in Harare, I moved across the airport to the small safari planes. A young girl was waiting to fly me to the Omay Camp up high on a cliff above the Omay River. After about a three-hour flight, we landed on the dirt strip high above the river. I was met by the camp manager. I noticed that he had a lopsided face, but I didn't say anything until we arrived at the camp. Believe it or not, there was someone else from my home state there as well, but he was through hunting and left the next morning. So I was the only hunter remaining on a ten-day safari. At dinner that night, I found out what was wrong with the camp manager. A large Buffalo was caught in a snare, and he broke loose and mauled the camp manager, nearly killing him. He told me that he was so sick that he still didn't know if he would live through the ordeal. They had flown him to Harare and saved him, but he was still very ill. There was plenty to eat but a lot of the staples such as cream, cooking oil, and other things that helped change the taste of food were gone. We were able to get fresh vegetables at a place called the oasis. Springs kept this place green, and it was used as a huge garden in the valley with tall bluffs above and lots of water. We traveled around huge acreages of national parks, but the roads were rough. We had flats on new rubber tires every day. We actually wore out an air pump.

Traveling in and out of the hunting areas, there were people selling carvings, and that would stand along the road and wait for someone to come and buy their goods. We started the safari on Lake Kariba, a huge lake that separates Zimbabwe and Zambia. The croc lodge was a beautiful place with bushes and flowers. There are tables that were used to sort sardines. The outfitter was a sardine farmer on Lake Kariba but had run out of diesel fuel. He was an ex-Tutsi control officer and a Dish TV customer. I was croc hunting on the water but keep overshooting the dollar circle on their head. Finally, we got out of the boat and fired a few shots and made some minor adjustments to the scope, and we were back out hunting. Crocs can see, hear, and smell, so if you are trying to sneak up on him, try not to step on a limb or watch the wind. Because it took so long and we didn't have one, we had to get on with the rest of the safari with hope of coming back later for a croc. This was classified as a dangerous game safari, so we had lion, buffalo, and sable yet to go. We hadn't seen any lions, and the buffalo were wild as a March hare. They would smell us and run back into the national parks. The ones we could sneak up on were not big enough in the horn bases. I did shoot a large female on the start for lion bait, and she had the biggest rack for a female so far in the camp. We saw elephants and lots of buffalo, many crocodiles, and Tsetse flies. I took a sable in the Chirza Camp through the gates into the Tsetse fly areas. Then we stayed pretty much out of those areas. The Tsetse fly as along tail with a stinger on the end. If they get you, it hurts. We never saw a lion. They have so much territory to roam, and it's difficult to find them.

One day, we were driving along. Two operatives for the camp came out of nowhere with ammo belts. One carried a shotgun and the other carried a machine gun. Their objective was to run poachers off the concession or kill them if they started a fight. We gave them rides several times. They just walk all over and look for trouble. They were heavily armed, and I thought how heavy the ammo must be let alone the size of the guns. We finally got a buffalo and decided to head back to forgo the lion hunt since we hadn't seen one since the two that were seen the first day. We hunted for them several days but always got to a camp after they had eaten somebody. One day, we found a baby buffalo that had its chest scooped out. Usually, a lion will eat the chest area first for the best parts. So we went back to camp and left to finish the safari on Lake Kariba. We had been in and out of the towns and the HIV areas where the women would go for treatments. Nobody felt good from a treatment, and since we were moving between areas, we would give some of the wives a ride to the hunting area where they lived. Returning to Lake Kariba, we resumed croc hunting. I found out some history of the original camp owners from Lebanon. The original owners were bombed and killed in Lebanon. If they were fighting over ownership, usually, they would be bombed and killed.

It was almost time to fly out again, and I got my croc after a couple of days. The outfitter made a deal in the meantime to buy diesel to get his sardine business going. When it was time to leave, I was headed to Victoria Falls, and another young girl flew in and picked me up for the flight to Victoria Falls. I spent an afternoon at the falls and taking my photos of both sides, Zimbabwe and Zambia. That evening, I had dinner and decided to stroll over to the casino out front where you turn on the street to drive to my hotel. On the way, I heard the hotel security calling someone but wasn't sure who as he spoke no English. He finally stopped me, and I found out that some American Highway Patrolman from Iowa had flown over for the day from South Africa. As they were walking along, one of them touched a Cape Buffalo in the dark. There were three or four of them on the sidewalk. The area between the hotels was dark, but you could see the lights of the casino up ahead. Large animals roamed freely between the two hotels, so the hotel offered another way to go around the walkway that was safer to avoid the big animals.

The next day was spent returning to Johannesburg, South Africa, for the return to London. I am glad I booked British Air, as SAA was on strike. At the same time, British Air was striking as well, and we had sack lunches for the trip. Arriving in London and low on fuel, we had to circle Heathrow for an hour or more, as the British were getting back online from the strike. Landing there, I spent the whole weekend seeing the sights of London. From the Queen's quarters to Holland & Holland and the Grenadier, I went to nearly every place in town. After a great weekend of sightseeing, I returned home. It took nearly a year to get my trophies home, but everything made it. I had sent my dirty underwear and satellite phone along with my treasures from Africa through the DHL office in Victoria Falls. About a month later, everything arrived.

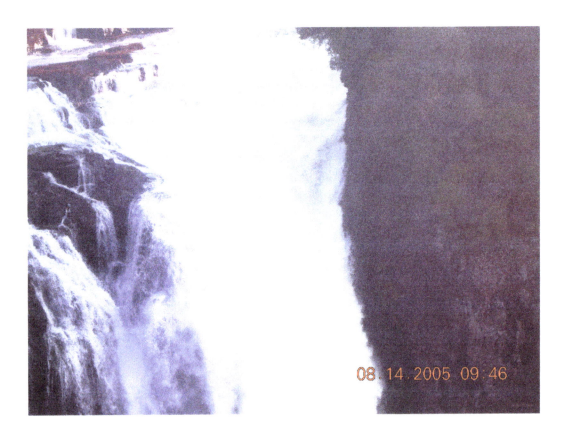

Victoria Falls side of Falls 2005

CHAPTER 14

Polar Bear Hunting on the Polar Ice Pack, 2006

Going from one extreme to another, this next trip was a real change in climate. Riding to Ottawa City in Canada for a one-day tour of the city was exciting, then a three-hour flight to Iqaluit and on to Resolute and a five-hour journey to the hotel. Snow everywhere, deep, brutal cold air. By the time I completed the ten-day polar bear hunt, hot water seemed like the only necessity that I needed. Raising my body temperature was more important than eating. The first three days, we got in a blizzard with seventy-five degrees below zero. Most of the trip was on rough ice. My arms felt like they were whipped rocking side to side on the rough ice and hurt for a month as I held on to the smoke stack of the mobile lodge while we maneuvered in and out of the jagged ice nearly turning over a few times. The ice had a greenish color, as it jutted through the four-foot ice stacked between us and the Arctic Ocean. We only saw four polar bears and no seals the whole ten days.

The outfitter told us a tale about ice that wasn't very comforting. If the wind direction turned a certain way, the ice could melt from the ocean nearly thirty miles inland from the water's edge immediately. We were about seventy miles. I rode to Iqaluit with a hunter from South Africa. He was hunting at Baffin Island about two hundred miles south of where Americans could hunt out of Resolute. About the third day, we heard there was a distress call on our radio from Baffin Island asking for immediate evacuation off the Arctic Ocean. The South African and the guide had camped the night before on what they believed to be a solid piece of ice. They woke up floating on the ocean approximately seventy miles an hour. They could barely see land from a sideview, as they were moving fast. They crashed into a solid piece of land or ice and jumped on to it. He went on to kill a huge bear. We rode back to Ottawa together, later talking about the trip. I continued hunting and sightseeing but did not get a chance at a bear. We continued on our journey through Lancaster Sound by Cornwallis Island, where the Franklin Expedition froze to death (there is a book about this called *Frozen in Time*). The guide showed us the place, and we spent several minutes talking about the expedition. On the way back to Resolute, we picked up a sled dog but lost two dogs the last night. A polar bear came close to camp and got in a fight with the two dogs. I don't know if they both made it back or not because I was out of there within the next few days.

I returned to Resolute finding that I shared the second floor with the Canadian military who was on maneuvers and taking photos of the polar ice. They showed me some photos of polar bears on north of where we were hunting. When I returned to Ottawa for the night and dinner with a fellow hunter, I was thinking about Resolute and what someone had said about the snow and ice melting and whether or not that Resolute would survive the thaw. As far as I know, they still exist on the polar ice pack.

CHAPTER 15

Second Dangerous Game Safari, Eighteen Days in Zambia, 2008

I arrived in Zambia in late June 2008 for an eighteen-day safari, spending the night in the capital and near embassy roll. They were all lined up along the highway, flags of every country. The next day, we took off for camp, as usual along the ride on dirt roads to the safari area. We were camped along the river in the North Luangwa Valley. The camp was very nice and had great food as well as lot of it. All of the food came from Somalia. We keep some strange hours while running the baiting cycle for eight days from one camp to another in the mountains. Sometimes we would spend the night in the mountains, and other times we were in the main camp. We received a barrel of fuel at the end of the week, and the outfitter remarked that my safari was burning more fuel and traveling many more miles than normal. We had to leave at 4:00 a.m. and travel to the bait areas till 10:00 p.m. some days. We had an option of hiring a cameraman to produce a TV show through a producer in the States. The cameraman lived close by in another country, so when he showed up there, it took some time to get used to having to talk into a camera; but after a day or two, it was like worrying about snakes. You kind of get over it or at least put the thought out of your immediate attention.

One afternoon, two black mambas came into the camp. The cook yelled to the outfitter to get his shotgun. They killed one, and the other got away. The cameraman went over and picked the dead snake up. I thought he was more man than I was. No way would I touch one of those. When I returned home a couple of weeks later, I was watching a TV show about the world's deadly snakes, and the first thing it said was not to pick up a dead poisonous snake, as the poison would still be in the skin. I never saw the cameraman again and wondered if he was still alive, although he made it through the safari. We were hunting for a lion bait and ended up taking a hippo first. When he went under the outfitter said, "Let's go back to camp, get a cup of coffee, and hire some guys to pull him out of the water." When we got back to the river, he was floating, and crocodiles were lying across the river on the other bank. At the same time, a group of Hippos were on their way to the dead Hippo upstream. Finally, the hired guys were able to boat out to the hippo and pull it to the bank. The outfitter pulled his vehicle close and winched the rest of the way out.

They collected the animal for trophy and bait. Having very thick skin, a lion will eat a few days on tough hippo skin. I wanted part of the hide, the skull, and ivories, so part of the hippo went to the ant eaters. As we would pull into the bait areas, I would lock and load my gun. I did that so many times I thought that my rifle would need replacement parts. Day after day, making this huge circle, we would replace bait as it was available. The next animal was a kudu, which we keep the trophy plus the back straps as the international preferred meat of any animal for the table. The rest went for lion bait, but a kudu doesn't last very long, so we continued to hunt to keep the lions interested. The next animal was a zebra. There were a lot of them in the safari area. We got a lion on the eighth day, and as we shot, the local conservation agents came in to take photos and congratulate me on my kill. The lions had been coming around their homes, and they had complained to the government about needing more hunters. They were armed, and we took a lot of photos of them with my lion. So now the pressure was off, and we could ease back. Shorter hours and the most dangerous part of the hunt was over, although we still had a buffalo to go. It turned out that I didn't see a bigger buffalo than I already had, so I wouldn't shoot one.

As we were traveling back and forth, we also did some burning. The grass was tall, and in Africa, you set a fire and don't worry about where it goes. I would estimate that I saw about one thousand buffalo, a few elephants, two leopards, two or three lions, and lots of zebra, giraffes, hippos, and crocodiles. There were also wild dogs and three black mambas, and I killed a bushbuck and a puku, only found in Zambia. The ants did a great job of cleaning the skulls in a short time.

One time after we camped the first time in the mountains, we were drinking coffee early in the morning, and a lion roared. We decided to investigate and see what the lions were doing. We got off the safari truck and walked through the tall grass. As we were walking in, a lioness walked within twelve feet of us in the grass. We started walking a little farther, and a lion roared about thirty feet in front of us. We quickly split up into two groups. The outfitter went one way, and I went the other with the head guide. The outfitter saw the lion first and said "do you see" in short words and kept repeating until I said "I don't see." Finally, after a few seconds, I said "do see," but the lion was in a low spot and could only see no shot, and away he went. There were three outfitters working out of the camp, my guide, a German, and one we called the third guide farmer.

One night during the lion hunt, we were approaching the camp, and a leopard walked in our headlights and almost to us. We were in a convertible. The outfitter had taken the top off his vehicle. The German told me that he thought that was dangerous to remove the top. One day in camp, the cameraman walked out of his tent, and there stood a four feet long Lizard. My outfitter was also sick with malaria, which is common in those areas where there is water. One day, we were hunting, and the president of Zambia was on his way home from a meeting in Egypt and had developed a sickness. That worried the staff, but you really don't get a lot of news on safari because you are so remote. So the eighteenth day came, and we were preparing to go back to Lusaka and then the trip to London and Chicago and then home.

CHAPTER 16

Caribou, Wolf and Fishing, Manitoba September 2009

This hunt was strictly an amphibious hunt. They dropped the planes into the middle of the lake, and boats came out to pick you up. Our lodge is on the border of North/South Dakota, and I started from there after a sixteen-hour drive from home. I spent a couple of days working around the lodge and then an eight-hour drive from there to the airport at Winnipeg. Next day, we were on our way north to Thompson and then north again to Egenolf Lake, named after a Catholic priest. The lodge was on the North Seal River System. We were probably an hour and half into flight, and weather would not permit us to go on in to land, so we returned to Thompson to have breakfast and wait for the weather to clear. They finally called us to take off again and began the last half of our flight into camp. The lodge had a private strip to go into, unpaved but large enough for big planes. We flew low, coming in as the cloud cover was still low level. At times it seemed like we would touch the uneven ground with the wings. Finally landing, we hiked to the lodge nearby; and as we approached, we saw the British flag flying above the lodge. The outfitter was a guitar player and had a small stage where he could play when they had time. But for about three weeks that had a window to hunt millions of caribou migrating to the US-Canadian border.

We flew out after a meal to each camp for the first night. I was headed to Camp Courageous and on to No Name lake. Circling the lake, I could see the platform in the middle getting larger. Boats came out to ferry us to shore. After a talk and look around, I went to my bunk and moved in for a few days. We would eat good food, including fresh fish out of the lake every day. Big fish and one of the best fishing trips I was ever on that you could catch Fish any time you went out. Breakfast every morning and then into the boats for a hunt. As I said earlier, an amphibious operation, without a boat, you would have to walk a long way around to get to where we went in a few minutes. There were lots of animals moving around, and several times, we were on the border of another territory within Canada. The pins or landmarks would always let us know where we were. My first caribou was fairly easy to take. There were so many that you could be over a hill and have a caribou walk by you. I either had an option to shoot two caribou or a caribou and a wolf. The problem with wolf hunting is that there are not many dead caribou carcasses to attract a wolf pack early in the season. So I opted to take another caribou in the velvet. I concentrated on more fishing while we waited to head back to the main camp with both of my caribou, and I flew out with two hunters from Nebraska. As we took off, there was not a caribou in sight. After they walked there, the pilot said they probably laid down to rest. Since they were headed to the US border, they had a long walk or swim. We were the only three hunters to complete our limit and had to wait a couple of days for everyone else to finish and return to camp. Staying at the main lodge, we fished and explored, looking for wolf and bear. I went out with a guide and fished in the big lake around camp while we waited. As everyone arrived, the small jet with a freezer on board picked up all the racks and meat for the return trip to Winnipeg. We boarded the big plane and headed back, but the pilot was showing an engine problem, so we had to make a landing in Thompson to put oil in one engine. Then we headed on to Winnipeg to part company and head home wherever that was. The two guys from Nebraska headed out and were driving all night. They told me to call the next morning, and they would tell me how crossing the border went. I spent the night and headed out early the next day but left the horns to be mounted in Winnipeg. Calling the other hunters on the way out, they had crossed the border with no problem, but a huge North Dakota white-tailed buck had come out of the sideview and went through their windshield, totaling their vehicle. I crossed the border and headed back to our lodge in the Dakotas for a day or two. Then after cooling the meat, I went back home in Missouri.

CHAPTER 17

North Island, New Zealand, 2010

I was a lucky hunter during this hunt. There were a variety of game to hunt and a scenic area to look for fallow, Arapawa Ram, wild turkey, hare, and set traps for crayfish. We hunted early and late and went out in the boat in midday to fish and trap for crayfish. The only thing that went wrong was the Iceland volcano went off at about the time I left the United States and sent a cloud of vapors across the planet. The only good thing was that it had to go a long ways to get to where I was in New Zealand. The family I was staying with had friends who were trapped in England, so we would come in at night and watch the news for updates. As we fished daily and ran the traps, the ocean was getting more violent every day. The volcano really upset the balance of nature. It finally got too rough to fish or trap, and there was an area toward shore that you couldn't go into because the waves were striking the shoreline. We would ride out in the boat, and you could see water higher than the boat. Then it would take the boat out on a wave and then drop the boat into a trough.

One day, we noticed someone in a uniform standing on the shore and investigating. He was an agent for the Marine Ministry. They were watching the water as it got wilder and bigger every day. Being on the south end of the Ring of Fire wasn't a very comforting thought, but by the time I finished my hunt to getting to the meetings on farther north, travel was not a problem domestically. I wondered if I would be able to jet home. This cloud that was between me and home was a disaster for aircraft it could damage the engines. I was able to hunt all the species that I mentioned earlier, and then I had to drive to another city in the north to fly on to Gisborne for the meetings. The outfitter's wife drove me to the airport, and I flew to the location of the meeting. I attended my meeting and began the process of international flight home. I could swear that the pilot changed the sound and throttled the engines back when we turned at the outer marker in Hawaii. It didn't take long to pick up the rugged coast of California and on into LA and Dallas and home.

CHAPTER 18

Australia, Hunting Buffalo, 2011

I decided to hunt the big buffalo on this trip. He was bigger than his cousins in Africa by five hundred pounds. He was much bigger, but the African buffalo is way more aggressive and meaner. If shot, he will attack what hurt him. They have been known to come from anywhere and attack. The wind plays an important part of a stalk. You can crawl right up to them if the wind is right; if not, look out. I was not only after the big one. The paperwork to fly to Taupo, New Zealand, and leave my weapon in the New Zealand Armory in Auckland for three days and then on to Gove, Australia, took a lot of work with permits to pull this off. I had Australian Police permits, a permit from the Australian Defense Department, and a dangerous goods permit from the airline. I spent three days in Taupo, New Zealand, sightseeing and going to the southern rim of the Ring of Fire, the volcano trail of the hottest, most explosive places on earth.

At the meeting I was attending, there was a well-known comedian there who more or less roasted the main owner of the project. A very funny guy. He even recognized me with a joke during the dinner. We had met earlier in the evening when he had arrived. The Taupo meetings were very informative, and I met some big corporations involved with company business in finance and insurance. I traveled the next day back to the Auckland Wharf by vehicle with another partner. I spent the night at the Wharf, and my favorite limo company and driver were picking me up the next day. He was an owner in the company and helped me pick up my gun at the armory. The agent waited while I checked in and then went away, and I did some shopping on the way to the gate. I entered Australia on the southern end at Sydney and flew all day to the northern airport at Gove. The outfitter met me, and we had a five-hour drive to camp. Arriving at the camp, I met the other guests from the United States and settled in for the night. The guests were from all over the United States and were making a short movie about hunting with primitive weapons in the outback. The next day, my guide and I took off for safari. I only had about two full days to hunt. We drove many miles before he found the right buffalo, and on the second day, we had a short stalk and long drive back with my buffalo. We did some fishing in the ocean the last morning. Huge Crocodiles, along with huge turtle shells, were lying on the beach. I talked the outfitter into traveling on to town in the evening instead of getting up real early, so I was there rested in time to board the plane to Melbourne, where I would spend the night. I arrived home from Australia with pneumonia and didn't know for a day or two until I got to feeling bad.

CHAPTER 19

Idaho Cow and Elk Hunting, August 2012

In August, the western fires were scorching the northwest at a rapid rate. I ran into fire traveling to Idaho starting in Montana. I was on the road heading through the Salmon area, and I remember the speed limit was seventy miles per hour. By the time I left the rest area in Idaho, the rangers said there was fire, but the tourists were traveling. The deeper into Idaho I traveled, the thicker the smoke. I got about halfway down the mountain cruising along when I saw an arm come up and a ranger motioned to slow down. I got a little farther and saw a fire crew on a side road and figured that I needed an update on the fire. The lady ranger told me the smoke and fire should reside some as I traveled a few more miles. When I got to where I was going, there was hardly any smoke, so the hunt was tolerable, but smoke was coming up the valley. It was only a matter of time until the whole valley was full of smoke. We shot an elk cow in the evening on top of the mountain. By the time we found her, it was dark. The guide said we will pull her down to the bottom and go get the truck to pick her up. We ran into down timber and hung the carcass up several times. Finally, at about ten o'clock, the guide decided to have the outfitter come and get us at the bottom because it had turned into a nightmare trying to navigate in the dark. By the time he got there and we got back to camp, it was dinner at midnight. I left out the next day with the elk carcass and decided to beat the fire coming down the valley, so I went west and north and got on the interstate in Northern Idaho, drove to Montana, had my meat processed, and headed out of Montana to North Dakota and to our lodge early in the morning out of the smoke. I stayed a day or two to freeze the meat and went home. My next elk hunting adventure was in August again and near the dinosaur area around Vernal. I got my cow early and I and other hunters began a trip through Crouse Canyon, Swallow Canyon, across the Green River to the John Jarvis Ranch, hideout for famous outlaws and their trail to elude lawmen. Overall, it was about an 8-hour trip by ATV.

Mike Honeycutt

CHAPTER 20

Hunting and Working, New Zealand, April 23, 2013

I returned to New Zealand for the forestry meetings and to do some more hunting for fallow deer. As usual, I set a seven-day return to the United States. I generally start a hunt and then move to the meetings from there. I left home and flew to Honolulu, Hawaii; Sydney, Australia; and Queenstown, New Zealand. From there, the outfitter, picked me up at the airport to the lodge north of Queenstown. I enjoyed hunting this area, as it was a picturesque view of the large lakes in the area. It took a couple of days to get my fallow. It was white in color. This was a great trip to sightsee and just go around and look at the scenery, and the hosts—or as I call them, outfitters—were a pleasure to ride and talk with. I still see them at the world show and stay in touch. We returned one evening for snacks and a drink of some kind. There was another couple from California, and we had some conversation, and I told the host that I was quite relieved that I could finally leave home, and there was nothing going on. No disasters and no violence at home. I went upstairs with a drink and sat down to watch the news. The big story was that someone had bombed the Boston Marathon. We continued to hunt but had to get to the meeting. From there, I got up early on the wharf in Auckland and was looking out at the bay while having breakfast. It was 7:19 a.m. I was checking my itinerary back into Honolulu and was scheduled there at the same time as I was having breakfast the same day. I said in an earlier hunt it is always better to return from the West than going West. I met my cousins, and we went all over Honolulu, did the museums and the pineapple store on the other side. It was a great tour of everything. I flew home after the weekend, which, by the way, is usually a no-no when you are on an international schedule, but the airline needed off, so they gave me the weekend off. I flew out of Honolulu on Monday afternoon, perfect ending to a great trip.

Mike Honeycutt

CHAPTER 21

Elk Hunting, Quebec, Canada, 2013

In the fall of 2013, I decided to go elk hunting. My freezers were empty and had no extra meat for the winter. There was a short flight and a three-day hunt on the property in Quebec about one hour north of Montreal. I flew to Chicago and about another three hours to Montreal. A driver picked me up, and we gathered luggage and on to the hunting lodge. We arrived and unloaded the cargo in about two hours. I did the usual on a safari by checking the facilities and the sleeping quarters area. After a while, we decided to go hunting, as I didn't have a lot of time to hunt. We did a lot of scouting, and it was pretty cold there. The elk kept going around and would cross after we would, so they were hard to see. The next day was spent trying to outsmart the elk and checking out different areas of the property. Finally, the last morning, we were hunting in a swamp and found a dead elk that had been poached. Also, we walked through the cold early morning to a hilltop and split up. One guide went another area not too far from us. Keep in mind this is the last morning. I was scheduled to fly out the next day, but a storm was approaching with high winds. As we walked to a point where I could see the valley, several head of red stag and elk ran down the fence line, and the guide yelled to shoot the elk in the down timber. He fell, and I got a nice bull. We headed to camp, had a breakfast, and loaded up for the airport. The flight was bumpy, and I landed in Chicago. I had Halloween dinner in Chicago and headed home.

CHAPTER 22

Botswana, September 2015, Elephant Hunt

I canceled this hunt because of timing and mostly that my wife was very ill with cancer. After surgery, there was a good prognosis. Plus, most of my immediate family was there as well. A few days later, the outfitter called and said that a hunter had canceled the dates that I wanted to return to Africa. I told her that I didn't think I could make the trip. I visited with the family, and they intended to stay. I had already been there several days, so they said. "If you want to go take off, we will watch Mom." My wife, more or less, went along since there were so many of us in the room. I called the outfitter back, and they began the process since it was short notice. It surprised me that it went as smooth as it did. I left the hospital the next day, drove twelve hours home, spent the next day getting ready, and flew to Switzerland the next and on to Botswana. I still don't know what happen after we left North America. The plane made some kind of correction or something in the air. Most people were asleep, but I normally stay awake. The plane suddenly went straight up in the air, then left, then right, and then straightened out. My stomach went left, and I had trouble the whole trip. Landing in Zurich, I decided to day trip around. I didn't plan on trains or people not speaking any English. It was a nightmare getting around. I took a couple of train rides and then went back to the airport for the flight to Botswana. The country was shutting down hunting in the northern national parks, so my hunt was one of the last. It was a long flight and even longer drive to the hunting area. I was glad to get there and eat a good meal. At night, you had to stay in your bungalow so the roaming lions didn't eat you. A waterhole was about one hundred yards away, and buffalo, giraffes, and lions roamed all night and day. We traveled every day and walked up on a lot of elephants. As long as the wind direction was right, we could walk right up to them.

In the north, where there was no river, the outfitter helped the conservation areas keep the wells going. We checked them every day. Saw lots of animals. One night, I think a lion caught something because it screamed in the night. The outfitter told me that when they all pull out, the government will have a real poaching problem. His feeling was that they would reopen to elephant hunters in a year or two, but the present regime was against hunting. They also were allowing some groups to continue plains game hunting, but who knows. I haven't checked on any more hunting there, and it is 2017, two years later. We continued the hunt and walked up to lots of elephants, but most were too small to hunt. One thing for sure, you can't hunt around the waterholes where they water. On the way out, I flew to the capital and spent the night. I was updating my iPad in the hotel lobby when some guys sit down beside me. They asked if I knew so and so, but I said no. When they left, I was thinking about the name, and the only thing that came to mind was a movie I had seen that name as a terrorist that attacked a shopping mall. Believe it or not, I tuned into the local TV station to watch the shopping mall attack in Kenya. How ironic it was that I thought of the same thing on a movie. I noticed when I was updating my iPad that the programs loaded different. My guide picked me up the next afternoon for the flight out to Zurich, and we stopped across the airport so I could eat a fresh fish sandwich at a restaurant on the corner. The food was good there, and I didn't lose any weight. I flew to Zurich and then headed home so I could get back to the hospital. There were still two weeks of radiation left for my wife's treatments.

Mike Honeycutt

CHAPTER 23

September 13-28, 2017

I just returned from another journey into Canada. I drove my vehicle about 2,700 miles to hunt for moose in the Queensland and National Forests of Canada in BC. The drive across the border was spectacular. The fall in Banff, Jasper, the avalanche area, was scenic and rugged. I saw elk and a grizzly in front of me cross the Trans-Canada Highway, and in the hunting area, I saw seven black bears. The hunting camp was only an hour out of town, but coming and going, you had to watch for the logging trucks, as they moved twenty-four hours, long trees and long rigs. Plus, they need a lot of road. They have a machine that mows those thick trees like you mow your lawn. We hunted hard daily, driving, walking, and scoping the openings. With fall almost at its peak, some of the fields had colorful grass. Since a lot of the trees are pine, you didn't see a lot of color, but there were areas that were more colorful than others. The countryside reminded me of Russia in fall. The terrain there is deceiving. There are deep ravines and down timber, but there is a lot of water flowing in the main stream that winds through a national forest. I didn't see many big animals, actually more bears than anything else. I was able to bring home a freezer full of moose, and my horns are ready for shipment. I drove my new GMC pickup. The outfitter asked me about my brand. I told him that my truck was 38 percent American/Canadian and the rest came from Mexico City. My truck came out of Mexico City with a group of diesel pickups to the final destination. With a good hunt and spectacular scenery and enough rain and weather to kill the massive fires south of us, the drive home only took three nights out. The smoke was gone, but instead of driving south to Yellowstone, the end of the Great Bear Trail, I drove the interstate to drive around the weather in the park and make time to the house. I was due into North/South Dakota for the opener of pheasant season, so I didn't spend much time off the road.

Mike Honeycutt

Chapter 24

Travel to Canada for a Fishing Trip in June 2004

Preparation and private plane travel to a foreign country does require some serious planning to meet the floatplane operator at the dock at a certain time. Actually, plane schedules of any kind are figured to the minute so that everything clicks at the same time. Fishing in Canada, when the Walleye are spawning, is considered very early just as the ice melts. Sometimes the weather is good, but at times there are adverse conditions, such as lightning and high waves, during a storm. Such was one trip in particular into Red Lake Ontario. We left early and arrived very early. Going into the airport, we had to go around again, as there was another jet trying to land at the same time. Even so, we arrived earlier than we ever had. We left at 7:30 a.m. and arrived at Red Lake at 9:30 a.m., cleared customs, and were picked up by the floatplane. We arrived at the camp by 11:00 a.m., had lunch, received our fishing licenses, and were on the lake by 1:00 p.m. That was a record for us, and with perfect timing, we fished all afternoon. Those trips don't always figure that smooth, but it gave us an early start for a three-day trip.

The bears were out, and we fished and were catching lots of fish. As the bear watched very hungrily from hibernation, he lay across a rock, and we would circle by and throw him a fish every now and then. He was one lucky bear. We were catching fish, and he was hungry. We had already caught our shore lunch for noon, so feeding a hungry bear was a side treat that you don't see every trip. Seeing bears was a common thing on the lake or in camp, but actually having one pose for a meal was entertaining. The lake is very big and over a thousand feet deep. When a storm stirs the water, the waves can come up to three to five feet.

One afternoon late in the evening, we were fishing and got hit by a heavy rain. The boat was filling up with cold lake water, and you could barely see the next boat over. We usually fished with several other boats, not far from shore but a freezing swim to the shoreline of the lake. As the boat filled up, the guide decided to speed up and pull the plug in the back, sucking the water out of the boat. In theory, this sounded like it would work, but we called the other boat over to us as we thought we might have to abandon ship. The boat continued to fill with water, and as it was getting dangerously full, the water suddenly gushed out, and the boat returned to normal as the heavy rain subsided. I was quite relieved, as I did not want to swim sixty yards to shore in large waves and frigid water; but with exception of a few minor blunders on the lake, we had a great trip. Another trip we flew in earlier than June in late May. There were storms during that trip, and because it was a week earlier, we were crossing the lake one morning while lightning was striking the water. Dodging the lightning strikes, we crossed the big channel into one of the side channels toward camp. Fishing there was usually very good, and we got to know the lake pretty well, but you couldn't second guess the weather. Usually, if you were out on the lake, it is when a thunderstorm would come by.

The best part of the whole trip and always recommended is the shore lunch. If you caught plenty of fish in the morning, you could have a great lunch that consisted of fish chowder, fried fish, and all the condiments such as a can of corn, baked beans, a can of tomatoes, or fried potatoes. We always ate good. If you ate a good lunch, usually, you could make it till dinner. The seagulls came by at lunch for pieces of fish, and because we would shore lunch on a deserted island, occasionally, a bear would wander into lunch to finish the meal. A few times, we would leave shore lunch in a hurry. You never had time to sleep or dose off because there was a hungry bear nearby. We always fished hard for three days and made good use of the boats in the evening after the guides quit for the day. After dinner, you were allowed to go out on our own and fish till dark. Three days comes and goes faster than normal, so the gear was hauled to the end of the dock along with coolers full of fish. The plane would pick us up and return us to the dock where we would ride to the airport for the return trip home. The floatplanes had been used in the war. They still had bombing switches on the dash, and some of them had holes in them from gunfire. The return to the United States was a short trip, and even though we were loaded with fish as well as gear, it didn't seem to slow us down unless we had a headwind. We would clear customs and head then home.

CHAPTER 25

In 2006, I decided to go south of the border. I know this one seems kind of different, but it just worked out that way. I had set up a trip to Vegas to try out an old motor home that my family decided to maybe sell. We had bought another vehicle that was newer and a little bigger to use for vacations and to haul people in our business, so they told me I could check it out on a trip already planned with my wife. Everything was ready to go. I made the reservations in Vegas. At the last minute, my wife backed out. Her mother wasn't well, so it was too close to check-in time, and I couldn't cancel the reservations. So after a talk with her, I decided to go alone, check out the motor home, and maybe fly from there to Costa Rica for three days and return to Vegas, pick up the vehicle, and return home.

The show I went to was a gun and hunting show that I have been to every year since. If you make reservations through the show, the rooms are a better rate, but try to cancel, and you get penalized for canceling the last minute. I took off for Las Vegas and, after a night out, entered the motor home parking where I would leave the vehicle for the trip. Checked in and proceeded to dinner and the casino for a while. I was tired from the all-day drive, so I went to bed getting up early to go to the show. I wanted to get an early start so I could see as much as I could before leaving early the next day for Miami and then on to San Jose, Costa Rica. It takes all day with time changes to Miami to make San Jose. Arriving in the evening, I checked in to the hotel and then out again to the airport the next morning. We arrived at the lodge in the afternoon for three days of fishing. They used Boston Whalers, had a new boat, great crew, and a roof to keep out the sun plus a toilet as well. The channel at the end of the dock lead to the Pacific Ocean. As you boated out of the channel to the ocean, the country of Colombia was south of us and Nicaragua was north. Out of the channel and into the ocean, it was a mile deep. It wasn't gradual; it was straight down from the channel. The Gulf of Dulce was the name of the body of water where the Lodge was located. I caught rooster fish, sailfish, and had a large Tuna or some kind of mammal that I fought for three hours and broke the line almost at the boat. The guide suggested that it was a tuna, but no one knows for sure. He said if we had got it in the boat and it was a Tuna, it would have paid for my trip to Costa Rica. There was no military in Costa Rica, only photos of NASA at the airport. The schools were taught by Nicaraguan teachers because they could make more money there. After my three days, I headed back to the airport for transport to San Jose to fly back to Las Vegas.

On the way to San Jose, we were riding along, and the plane suddenly flipped sideways and then returned to normal. The lady in front of me was hurt, probably a whiplash from the sudden flip. Other than that, the flight was smooth. I boarded the jet in Miami and began the long ride to Las Vegas. It was really dark all the way till a turn the pilot made on the last leg of the flight. Phoenix was south and lit the sky, and Vegas was lit up to the north. Landing at Vegas, I returned for the night, picked up the Motor Home the next morning, and headed into seventy-mile-an-hour winds in Winslow, Arizona. I drove through Winslow with my steering wheel turned sideways. It was like flying a small plane in a crosswind. Fought it for miles before the wind died down and returned home.

CHAPTER 26

In May 2009, I decided to go back to Canada. This trip was on the Alaskan Highway about eight hours from Alaska and in the northern part of British Columbia on Muncho Lake. It was several segments of flight through Vancouver to Dawson Creek to Fort Nelson and then about a three-hour drive through the Stone Sheep Park to the lodge that services passengers passing to and from Alaska. When I drive the Alaskan Highway, I will stay there for a few nights. The lodge is in the northern part of the start of the Rocky Mountains, very scenic and rugged, steep and snow-covered. When I was there, some of the small lakes were still frozen. Landing on one lake, you could see the fires in the Yukon. We proved a point about lift and airplanes on one lake. We flew two floatplanes together, and we tried to take off on a long arm of one lake with the wind; and there was no way it would lift, which is what we thought would happen. So we turned around and lifted off. We fished a different lake every day. One place we wore waders, and I was in the water fishing up to my waist catching fish. I turned and walked the trail to the river and was fishing along the bank. The outfitter was carrying a double barrel in case there was bear trouble. I realized that everyone had walked back to the plane, so I turned from the river and was walking along to the trail and nearly stepped in a huge pool of blood. I stepped it up to the plane, but nobody had seen that pool of blood. I still wonder what that was from. I brought fish back from that trip, and we had two good fish fries at home. I fished with several different people on that trip, and with the scenery and company, we had a great time.

Stone Sheep Crossing Alaskan Hwy

CHAPTER 27

Another Trip South of the Border to the Amazon Region

This trip started in November 2009. I took a flight to Atlanta, Georgia; Miami, Florida, and Manaus, Brazil, and spent the night in Manaus waiting for transport to the Rio Negro Lodge. The fishing trip was on that Rio Negro River that flows parallel to the mighty Amazon River. This trip was the last trip out of the lodge. It had been open for years, but because of hard times, it was closing after this last trip. There were lots of people there. Some rich fisherman from Mexico, doctors from the States, and a lot of other Americans go there to catch the famous peacock bass and a few piranhas. I had signed up single after watching the video and paid extra for my own boat. In the video, it shows a guy fishing, and I know him, hooking another fisherman with one of the huge lures that you fish with. One, I didn't want to fish with a stranger; and two, I was not used to throwing a large lure on a sixty-pound test line, so I was afraid that I might hook someone with the lure, and, boy, would that hurt. You can imagine a regular lure with hooks and triple it in size. We arrived and went to our rooms. There was blood on the sidewalks, and I asked the host where that blood came from. He told me that they were pretty sure that a jaguar had eaten a couple of monkeys just before we arrived, so we secured our rooms for the night, and they were made of solid concrete and steel doors to keep the bugs out. There were lots of insects and bushmaster snakes around, and they said it was unlikely that if we got lost in the jungle, we would survive the night.

The walkways were dim lit, and sidewalks to the main lodge were narrow. Beautiful place just carved out of the jungle. It was actually a city in itself. They had a school and dental and medical facilities. All kinds of buildings and paintings. It was a shame that they were closing down. There was a yacht that was moored to one of the docks that they had used for overnight fishing trips. We did a tour one day and looked at the different parts of the complex and also a nature walk to taste the raw form of gum that makes chewing gum.

Fishing was great. I caught a lot of fish, and as the only single team, I caught the most fish for the week and one of the biggest. I have a replica of it on my trophy room wall. At night after a full day of fishing, we would return and clean up, have a drink, and get ready for dinner. One night, I came by for a drink and had a minor scratchy throat, so I returned to my room to take an antibiotic. When I returned, some of the men were at the bar talking about a machine gun nest at a road that was closed in a foreign country that a group of doctors tried to go through and the gatekeeper wouldn't let them pass. I am sure that it is the one that I wrote about in my earlier story about Tajikistan from the way they described the area. They were mad that they were not allowed to pass. I don't know if they were hunting or working, but the guard would not let them through, and you could only pass in the daylight. At night, the highway was used by drug smugglers, and it was dangerous enough that they had a huge machine gun post there. The guard sits right behind the machine gun and steps down to open the gate.

I signed up for shore lunch every day. We would break late morning from the bass fishing to catch piranhas for lunch. The guides would find a place to eat and build a fire and a grill out of sticks and score and place bass and piranhas on the grill to cook. Actually, the piranhas tasted better than the bass. Different from the movies as we ate the piranhas versus the piranhas eating the people. That was an eight-day trip, so I caught many fish and explored the river system.

One day, we were in a small stream, and the guide had to get out of the boat because we were hung up on a log. As he was moving the boat, I was looking around on the little island west of where we had come through the narrow channel in the river. In the darkness on the island, I looked into two big glowing eyes watching us from the shore. It must have been a large jaguar in the jungle had stopped to look and see what was going on. He turned and moved away from us and disappeared in the thick jungle cover. We continued on to fish until it was time to catch piranhas for lunch. Returning to Manaus, we had another overnight and began sightseeing around the city and the open market. There were soldiers all over the city. I asked the cab driver why there were so many soldiers, and he said that it was the northern defense force between the jungle, Colombia, and Venezuela. He said there was about four hundred thousand soldiers there, which made the city seem crowded but like most big cities. We spent all day and went out to dinner and returned to the hotel to begin packing for the journey back to the States. I came downstairs in the morning to find police everywhere. One of the fisherman had accidentally ripped the door knob off a van, and the cab driver turned him in to the police. Two squad cars full of police had the counter surrounded and the man that ripped the door knob behind closed doors at the hotel. After a while, he came out and had to pay for the door knob before he could leave the country. We left for the airport to head home and, after a long flight, returned to south central Missouri.

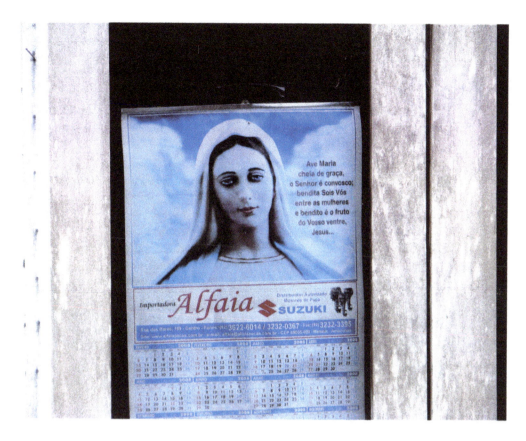

ACKNOWLEDGMENT

In finishing this short hunting, fishing, and adventure story around the world, I would just like to say that I want to thank the world outfitters, travel agents, and border protection people who helped me through these excursions with gear and weapons and hope to do some more traveling soon. Also, I would like to dedicate this short story to my wife, who died in 2016, and to my Australian outfitter, who died last year.

CPSIA information can be obtained
at www.ICGtesting.com
Printed in the USA
BVHW02s1308290618
520433BV00020B/624/P